How to Plan a Successful Fundraising Dinner:
The Dinner Committee Handbook

Phil Wood

DEDICATION

To Wayne Greenawalt and James Lukose
for showering me with opportunity, wisdom, and encouragement.

CONTENTS

ACKNOWLEDGMENTS

Thank you to all the Dinner Committee Members who have sat through years of planning; labored through hours of set-up, hosting, and disassembling the events; and for being fellow advocates of the great causes that unite us.

1 TAKING THE LEAP

We have exceeded our fundraising goal, was the first announcement of the Master of Ceremonies over the buzzing portable sound system in the crowded hotel meeting room. We had just finished dinner, gave a small presentation, and collected pledge cards. Unfortunately, the cheers were then interrupted with awkward silence and an apology for miscalculation. Now it appeared we were actually substantially under.

After the three young professionals in the front of the room at the folding table conferred again, it seems the accurate total was closer to the first then the second. The crowd once again cheered, but that little snapshot is just an example of a few of the snafus of the evening.

My first attempt at organizing a fundraising dinner was a fiasco. We could not have done more things wrong, yet we still ended with respectable results. I cannot imagine how things would have turned out if we would have known what we were doing.

On that evening we were launching a million dollar capital development campaign that exceeded many times over our annual budget. In preparation, we secured a banquet room at the local hotel and picked the menu for the evening. That was about the extent of our pre-planning. Even our program lacked substance, yet when the pledges came in we miraculously reached our goal for the evening. We were so excited yet so pathetic that we could not even get an accurate total.

A few years later, my next involvement in a fundraising dinner came during the first week of the first month in my new role as a Director of a not-for-profit organization. My very first public appearance in that position was actually an annual *Friendship Dinner* that had been planned for months. I should have realized right then it was an omen. While I thought I accepted the position to help people, or at the very least, help the people who help the people, it soon became clear my primary objective was to raise money to keep the organization solvent.

Those two nights began a journey that has forever shifted my view of how to fund charitable organizations. It also began my love-hate relationship with the Annual Fund-Raising Dinner.

I left the event that evening feeling the same way I have at every one since. First, exhausted. There is little to compare to something that takes so much work for such a brief period of time. Second, overwhelmed. Every year I wonder, "How on earth can we top this next year?" But third, energized. Not only is it always a nice evening for everyone involved, but I have a whole new pool of friends. Many of them I will get to know personally, some will actually volunteer in our organization or on our board, and most will support what we are doing for many years.

In our situation with a grass roots volunteer-heavy organization, I cannot even begin to imagine what could take the place of the Annual Friendship Dinner for raising revenue and raising new friends. The hardest part is getting one started, but once it is up and rolling, it is hard to hold back the momentum.

Agenda Item:

1. List reasons why we should or should not plan a fund-raising dinner for next year.

2 DO NOT ATTEMPT THIS ALONE!

I call my romance with dinners a love-hate relationship because I love the results, but I am not so fond of the process. It is plain hard work. For that reason alone, many organizations and organizational leaders never attempt a dinner and others kill the ones that have been like fixtures in the life of an organization. They do not think it is worth the effort.

It is also difficult to let your true intentions be known. It is a fund-raiser. While friends are made, this dinner is to raise income. You can plan dinners to honor volunteers, to celebrate milestones in the life of the organization, or to spread awareness for the cause, but successful fund-raising dinners are not ambiguous. You, along with everyone involved, must know why it is planned.

To get it rolling, you need a group of committed people. Before you pick your date, venue, or theme, pick your team. Hopefully your organization has already groomed people that have a commitment to your cause, have sweat equity in your organization, have established some level of camaraderie, and are people of influence. They do not need to be people of means, but they do need to be people of influence. Wall flowers will not get the job done.

There is a tendency to hire someone from outside the organization or appoint someone from within to make the dinner happen. Can you say, *Failure and Frustration?* This is how it usually works: Learning how dinners have generated substantial income for other organizations, the Executive Director convinces the board, or vice-versa, they need their own event. At that point, to either support the E.D. or to placate her, they task the development director or otherwise approve a new hire. One person, however, will not get this huge boulder rolling. One person may ignite the spark, but for it to be executed well it is going to take a small army.

Your board is your natural launching committee. If you have recruited well, you already have the right type of people and if you have trained well they know about their fiduciary responsibility. They need to have skin in the game and be motivating others to do the same. If they are not doing this, does the board have other clearly defined roles instead?

Ten people are all you need to launch. Assuming you are heading it up, you need one person that is all about organization, keeping all the facts straight and remembering all the specifics; you need a couple of people that are into hospitality and care about details like centerpieces and name tags; and you need five or six people that will fill the hall.

With a core of ten people, your first dinner or gala can easily launch with 100 guests. Most of your initial 10 have mates or significant others that they can influence to come, giving you close to 20 attendees for your event before you even go public. Of the six or seven movers and shakers on your board, each one of them can fill a table of eight or ten, which essentially means merely inviting three or four other couples out for the evening. Once again, if your board members cannot exert that much influence to motivate a few other couples to join them to support an organization that they are so passionate about that they are willing to serve on the board, they either are not really passionate about the cause or they are just not passionate, and thus not really influential. This event is a chance for them to put shoe leather to their talk.

One word of caution is that key volunteers or staff are not always the best individuals for these roles. While you might have leverage to coerce, force, or even guilt them, you might be trying to cram a large round peg into a small square hole. People volunteer for many reasons and hours clocked with an organization does not always qualify one to become a spokesperson or representative. Another rule of thumb is that in a grass roots type organization, volunteers do not give and givers do not volunteer. It is often a myth that involved people give more. Involved volunteers may give more than those not involved in serving in the organization, but they generally do not give substantially. The largest donors may never enter the doors of your organization, and if they do, they may never enter twice. They give because they trust you and believe in your cause.

Additionally, of the five or six people on your core group, at least two or three of them know of at least one person that has enough pull and influence to gather a table of their own. All total, you now have about ten table hosts and hostesses attempting to round up another 80 people for a nice little event. Depending on the dynamics, resources, and history of the organization, you can take the risk and go large on year one and launch with a bigger bang or you can begin to build the foundation, getting the flywheel in motion, aiming for year three as the year to really go public. A huge launch will rely on celebrity appeal and creative marketing to make a splash and a slow grow might creep out of the station, but can build steam quickly and will probably be harder to stop in the long run.

Agenda Item:

1. What is a realistic attendance goal for next year's event?
    _____

2. Divide the goal by 10. List one person of influence for each grouping of 10 who is committed to your organization or cause and who can be approached to take responsibility as hosts/hostesses.

3 PICK A DATE, BUT NOT ANY DATE

Now that you have a team in mind, invite each member to a planning meeting. If the team is already intact such as a board, build it into one of your already scheduled meetings. Unless you have a super efficient board that has clear purposes and full meeting agendas, there is probably time in your regular meeting to plan out the dinner event.

Assuming they have already bought into the goal and do not need to be persuaded to even have the dinner, the first item on the agenda is to pick the date. Your agenda for the first meeting does not need to be much, but by all means, nail down the date. Nothing will solidify the event and begin to turn a dream into a reality like putting a stake in the ground and confirming the date.

Because there are plenty of people that are in business to profit from making things happen, you could pull off any event almost overnight. Not wanting to just pull it off, but rather to get the most mileage out of the evening, you need a minimum of eight months.

Keep in mind, it is not just about the event, but it is about using the event to promote your cause and organization. Mailings prior to the event, public service announcements, press releases, and follow-up newsletters can create a whole new image for your organization. You do not want to miss out on all the free PR and mileage this event can bring.

Unless there is a connection to a time of the year that really makes sense for your organization, why would you want to do the summer months when people and their money are on vacation; back-to-school time when schedules get crazy; the end of the year and around the Christmas holidays when people are going to give to you naturally; the dead of winter when no one wants to go out; or late spring when weddings and graduations are crowding the calendar and emptying the wallet?

That leaves the sweet spot of March through early May, depending upon that year's date for Easter, or late September into early November. Wanting to have an event that nails down a yearly time slot, because of the floating nature of Easter, you may want to stay clear of the spring. On the other hand, October has become a major wedding month, but unless your circle is small and someone significant is getting hitched, I doubt a few weddings will derail your event.

The next challenge is not conflicting with established events of other favorite charities. Your board members may be sitting on other boards or volunteering with other organizations or there just may be a major dinner that gets a bunch of attention each year in October. Why fight it? The pie can only be sliced into so many pieces. Pay attention to the patterns for dinners and galas of other, like-minded or local organizations, and try to work with them, not against them. In fact, you may want to even start attending their events to begin creating reciprocal support and encouragement. If nothing else, you can see what is working effectively in other settings.

Assuming you have picked a time of the year, the night of the week can make or break your event. Of course, one huge factor includes venue availability. If you happen to be teetotalers, banquet halls will love you on Tuesday night but are loath to schedule a dry weekend banquet. A dry event may not even be able to get a nice venue on Friday or Saturday evening.

Another factor includes the demographics and commuting patterns of your likely guests. If it is an older group that tends to be retired, a Tuesday or Thursday evening could work fine. Depending upon the religion or the religiosity of your group, anything from Friday evening, Saturday, Sunday, or Wednesday can pose challenges. If you are in the suburbs of a major city or inner-city with suburban supporters, a weeknight might make the commute pretty challenging.

Unless you are in the territory where high school football reigns and families are heavily involved, there is probably no more prime time to plan a dinner than a Friday evening in mid-October. Remember, this is a fund-raiser. People with disposal income who can support your cause are probably not ones that need to worry about babysitting or even getting their own child off to the game. Most likely, empty nesters and beyond will carry the night. Even the heavy hitters, the ones who can really make the night a success, will probably attend a dinner about as much as they volunteer. They might attend a big gala, but do not be surprised if they snub a fund-raising dinner. Significant donors typically do not volunteer nor attend dinners. They can be very valuable team members, however, in making the evening an overall success.

Go ahead and nail down a date that works with the rhythm of your organization, the culture of your community, and the convenience of your team. If it works for them, it will probably work for your friends.

Be flexible, however, because this is where it gets tricky. Your venue may have limited availability and the date may impact who you can or cannot get for a speaker, entertainment, or music. You may nail down a date, knowing that it might be changed three times before it is finalized.

Agenda Item: Pick three dates that you think would be ideal and rate them in order of preference:

1. Preference Number One:

   _____

2. Preference Number Two:

   _____

3. Preference Number Three:

   _____

4 LOCATION, LOCATION, LOCATION

It is rumored that our organization's first organized dinner was a volunteer appreciation night in the basement of a church. While it barely broke even, it seemed to accomplish its intended function that evening. Even more than just honoring the faithful volunteers, however, it launched the Annual Dinner.

Would we choose a church basement again? Maybe, but it better be a nice one. Nothing makes a statement about the values of your organization like the facility in which your event is held. Too dumpy, and you lack the class to really connect with the type of donors you need and the type of environment to which they are accustomed. Too nice, and you are being extravagant and not good managers of their donations.

Once you are armed with a date, begin to shop your possibilities. Professional banquet halls are easy to work with, anxious to add to their numbers, even at a late date, and not rattled by the normal challenges of such a gathering.

On the other hand, non-traditional space such as halls at a church can be donated or discounted. Be careful, however, because what you gain in free space you may lose in extra costs to cater the dinner. These spaces typically do not come with staff, and if they do, these individuals are not accustomed to hosting dinners multiple times each week.

While you primarily need a venue that is large enough, easily accessible for those with mobility challenges, and with plenty of parking, you also want a place that is appealing to those in attendance. A museum, zoo, or other public facility that rents out space can be interesting enough for people to want to attend, just for the sake of the venue. Even what is lost in pizzazz can be gained in intrigue.

Space is easy to calculate. Overall, you need about 15 square feet for each person in attendance to accommodate the tables, room to walk around, and a stage. By way of comparison, 20 square feet per guest would be needed if you were planning a event like a wedding with a stage, dance floor, and table seating. On the other hand, a dinner with just reception type seating around tables with little room to move around needs only 10 square feet per person. If you are launching with a goal of 100 guests, your room should have about 1500 square feet or a room that is about 50' X 30'.

Tables work off a similar formula. The most common tables to use or rent are the 60" round table which can accommodate 8 to 10 guests. The next step is the 72" round which accommodates 10 to 12. Keep in mind that the larger the table you use the fewer tablecloths and centerpieces you have to make, buy, or rent. Ideally, your dinner of 100 will have 10 round 72" tables with 10 guests at each table.

In addition to size, when you pick the venue you have to consider the availability, cost, and feasibility of:

- Catering options
- Lighting
- Platform/stage
- Audio-Visual options including a video projector and sound system
- Entry and accommodations for coats or umbrellas
- Room for displays or book tables
- Restrooms
- Room layout, guest's proximity to stage, visual barriers such as posts or odd shaped rooms

By the time the event is confirmed, you will probably need to sign a contract, or at the very least prepare a detailed email outlining your intentions for the evening. If you are dealing with a banquet hall or a group that normally allows outside groups to use their space, they will have a contract. If your location does not require a contract, be very leery, but try to subvert any potential issues by clearly outlining what you had discussed and agreed upon. Your letter should contain what time you can get in to start decorating, what spaces and resources are available, how things will be set up and how they should be left, what the parameters are for decorating, and what are the costs.

As a final note, plan on securing an Insurance rider for many of the venues, particularly those that are not solely in the business of hosting dinners or those that are letting you use the space for free.

<u>Agenda Item:</u>

1. Collect suggestions for a venue, assigning team members the task of checking out the various facilities for feasibility and reporting back

5 TO CHARGE OR NOT TO CHARGE

For months, I heard a buzz in the community about a new documentary that was being produced for a local organization that provided tattoo removal or reconfiguration for those involved in the sex trafficking industry. Everyone I spoke with was excited about the project and looking forward to its release.

Finally, plans were announced to debut the newly produced documentary at the local theater, an ornately decorated 100-year-old venue that seated upwards of 1,000 people. Nearly packed, I sat midway back, near the aisle for a quick escape after the video ended. What I did not realize, however, is that there was not to be a quick escape.

Following the interesting and intriguing documentary, the director and those involved in production provided a live panel for upwards of an hour, talking about the experience of making the film. While it seemed to drag on and attendees fidgeted in their plush red theater seats, few moved from them.

Then, nearly two hours into the evening, the pitch came. After all the festivities, the chairperson of their board shared his plans, which was basically to give everything in his pocket to an offering that evening. He suggested that everyone in attendance do the same.

Unfortunately, I hardly ever carry cash and by the looks of it when the embarrassingly empty collection plate passed my lap, most other people do not either.

While I somewhat resented being held hostage for well over two hours, even more so I regretted not being able to participate in the collection. With all the buzz about the event, all that was mentioned and promoted was that it was free. Bus loads of church groups from the whole region arrived at the theater, but I cannot imagine many were prepared to share.

While the ambush may or may not have been intentional, I have to believe it backfired. In spite of that, I still left the evening moved for what they had accomplished and intending to make a donation someday. Unfortunately, up to this point, it has not happened. I just wish they would have let me know what they were planning. At a minimum, I would have brought a $20, maybe a $50 or $100, or possibly even a check. All I had in my wallet that evening, however, was a plastic debit card, and my potential donation stayed there.

In your planning, one huge decision is what to charge. The obvious options include either making the event free and trying to get donations once inside; charging a minimal amount or getting sponsors, still intending to upsell guests at the event; or simply charging a generous ticket price to attend.

In the preplanning, a huge decision that will greatly impact the success of the evening is how you are planning to raise funds.

One option is to offer a free dinner, intending to rely solely upon donations. In this case, try not to add confusion by the temptation to throw in silent auctions or raffles. Keep things very simple. The right people are invited to a free dinner with the intention that they can give from their hearts. The program is a gift to them and an encouragement for why they should give. The tax deduction is limited to the gift minus the value of the dinner. While there is risk with this approach, the upside potential is unlimited.

A second option is to charge for the dinner an amount that covers the cost of the event and the intended revenue goal. Several years ago a tall ships outing was planned for a group of nearly 100. The cost per person for the boat ride, dinner, and drinks was about $60. The cost per couple was $500. The big challenge here was selling all the tickets. Everyone went into the night, however, knowing what to expect and not fearing being guilted into having to give more. The weather turned out perfect and the evening turned out to be a very positive emotional experience.

Another option is a hybrid that assures the basic costs of the evening are covered but allows for upside once the event begins. Tickets are sold or individuals and tables are sponsored. Then, the night is full of auctions or fun ways to give.

As is true of most things, you are not selling the steak but you are selling the *sizzle*. A fund-raising gala or event is a chance for folks to have fun, enjoy a great experience, and be generous. The free dinner with an offering, in its purest form, is a chance for people to show the purest form of generosity and support.

As a side note, most accountants will remind you that anything tangible that the donor receives must be deducted from their overall gift.

Ultimately, to charge or not to charge is really determined by the culture of the organization, the community, and the overall goals for the evening.

<u>Agenda item:</u>

1. What strategies should we employ to make certain we cover the expenses of the event and turn it into a profitable use of our energy and resources?

6 PROGRAM & ENTERTAINMENT

In order to get the guest speaker or entertainment that you think will best enhance the evening, you may have to begin with their availability. Our largest dinner happened to be the evening we invited a country and western singing group from Colorado that just so happened to have a cult following in the Midwest. Even right up to the night of the dinner, people were phoning to see if they could still attend. That year, we started in our planning first with the entertainment, which determined which night we could even host the event. Lastly, we sought out a venue.

Assuming you are starting with a date and venue and then seeking a speaker or entertainment, you may not be able to get anyone that will draw a crowd, especially if the dinner is smaller or just starting out. The right speaker, which is basically someone that is well known and recognized, and is somehow connected to your cause or organization, will make it easy for hosts and hostesses to invite their guests. All of a sudden the pitch goes from, *Hey Joe, this organization that I help with is having a dinner, would you attend,* to the little bit easier ask of, *Joe, our organization is having a professional athlete or well-*

known personality this year and I know you would want to hear him.

If you are down to the six to eight month planning timeframe, you are getting close so do not be scared to swing for the fence. Well known speakers can be booked years in advance, which often comes at a significant pricetag, or sometimes at the last minute, which can be like a fire sale. We have booked some speakers two years in advance and others were finalized in the last two months.

Realistically, you will have to pay for a good speaker or musical artist, but you probably do not want to exceed 10% of your gross anticipated goal. In a day when speakers can command hundreds of thousands of dollars for a 30 minute speech, who do you think you can get for a $250 speaker's honorarium? If you cannot get someone that is widely known, get someone that is good and going to make for an enjoyable evening.

You want the evening to be a gift to all in attendance and for them to leave encouraged. Like a snowball, your guest list should grow each year and it should include the people from the previous year along with their guests. You want them to leave wanting more. Organizations that try to save the effort and money of securing a good guest speaker, musician, or entertainer will not only miss out on donations, but will lose the residual value of people looking forward to next year's dinner.

There is no harm is asking anyone and everyone, regardless of their stature, that might have a heart for your organization or cause. There is harm, however, in not getting someone that will make the guests want to laugh, cry, and emotionally identify with the cause.

Resist the temptation to believe that people are only coming to hear about your organization. Not true. They do not want to be tortured with statistics, kudos to hard working volunteers that they do not know, and bloated videos.

The best way to get a good speaker is to talk with someone that has connections. Leverage their relationship to a speaker by having them make the request. Additionally, if possible, have the speaker's honorarium and any travel expenses covered by an interested individual or corporation. It keeps the drama down when someone else foots the bill, especially when the speaker comes with a high pricetag. Guests can be put off to know that much of their donation is going toward the speaker's expenses.

The perfect combination for a speaker is well-known and entertaining. If you cannot get the well-known, go for the entertaining. If you cannot find entertaining and interesting, keep looking until you do.

<u>Agenda Items:</u>

1. Who are possible speakers, entertainers, or musicians that could join us for the evening?

2. How much can we budget for the speaker?

3. List individuals and corporations that might be willing to sponsor the keynote speaker or entertainment portion of the program:

7 THE THEME

Assuming you have the date, venue, and entertainment secured, you can now take a deep breath. Depending upon how far out you are, it may not be a very long breath, but you do have a bit of the hard work behind you.

Now you need to consider the theme of the evening. This will shape how you promote, how you decorate, and how you tie the evening together. In one sense, what theme you pick is not as important as just picking a theme. Since there are a lot of moving parts, it helps to clarify what everyone is working toward and it keeps the evening from looking like a patchwork quilt.

The theme is basically your battle cry. "Remember the Alamo" is a rallying cry that is hard to forget. It contains an imperative and a call to action. Religious groups can pull out a theme verse from the Bible or secular groups can draw from popular culture.

With a theme, the decorating team has fun coming up with ideas that support the theme. They will consider what the platform might look like, how the centerpieces on the tables connect and even how the colors of tablecloths support the one theme. Obviously, some themes are easier than others and have more options available.

It also gives structure to the graphic designers. When they begin producing copy and images for your save-the-date cards, your invitations, or even banners on the night of the event, the theme gives them direction.

This is also true for the speaker. While their one or two speeches may not change much from location to location, a polished speaker will try to make it fit your particular evening and event.

Once it becomes clear that your dinner is going to become a reality, everyone will step forward with suggestions. The agreed upon theme will begin to reel in the ideas, allowing everyone to be on the same page and focusing on one event.

The theme is like the blueprint that gives direction to the construction. On the night of the evening, some people may not even recognize the theme or all the effort you put into tightening up the event. If it is any comfort or consolation, they would probably notice had you NOT.

Agenda Items:

1. Suggested themes for the evening:

2. Suggested "rallying cries" to support the theme:

3. Suggested colors or images:

8 THE MENU

The other part of the pre-planning that can take place months in advance is the actual meal. It may have been a package deal with the venue or you may be seeking out a caterer separate from the location. In either case, it needs to be booked as early as possible.

The three basic options for serving include a buffet line where people serve themselves, family-style with large dishes served at each table, or individual plating. The cost for family-style or individual plating is about the same, given it takes about the same number of servers. Buffet lines are the least expensive, but you also have the challenge of older individuals trying to make their way back to their seat, juggling a cane in one hand and their plate in the other. Additionally, if the plates are flimsy, it could really create a scene.

Overall, people like being served, not having to pick their own portion, and not having to get up. The one advantage of family style is that it will save food should you want to provide something for those serving or if your organization happens to have a feeding program. At times we have had choirs singing or athletic teams from local colleges serving, and they tend to eat after everyone else is finished. The extra food that is available from family style serving keeps down the cost of having to order extra pizzas or meals for them.

It is going to be hard to firm up your final number until the last week. It is always strange, but on the actual night of the event at least ten percent of the people will not show. People get sick, have accidents, get called out of town, or plain forget, so while you do not know will not show, you can be sure at least ten percent will not.

I will explain later, but to try and avoid confusion on the night of the event I try to negotiate about ten percent more salads than the other portions of the meal. Some caterers will give push back on this, pricing everything for complete meals. It actually saves them work and confusion, plus they make a few more bucks on salads.

Hors d'oeuvres are an option, but not worth the extra cost for a dinner event. With the dinner being served promptly and many people rushing to get there, extra food is just an extra cost.

You definitely want rolls on the table and the meal to begin with salad or soup. With people arriving at varying times, salads have a longer table life and provide more perceived choices when a couple of different dressings are available at the table.

As far as sides, such as vegetables or starches, go with the caterer's specialty and recommendations. They know what works and what does not work, what people eat or leave untouched, and what gets rave reviews or complaints.

For the main course, the caterer may have a favorite here as well, but be aware that it has been reported by many in the field that a good beef meal results in higher donations than chicken. You probably do not want to spring for filet mignon, not wanting to give the wrong impression, but you probably want to "beef it up" and make it the nicest meal you can at the best value.

The same is true with desserts. For just a little more cost you can offer a dessert that is exquisite and memorable. There is nothing that will prepare someone for the program to follow like a cup of coffee or tea served with a favorite dessert. If you are going to skimp on the price, the place to cut costs is probably not in either the main course or the dessert.

Agenda Items:

1. Pick two or three qualified individuals who will sit with the caterer and plan out the menu for the evening.

2. Suggestions for those who will decide upon the menu:

9 TIMELINE

One year, even just weeks before the event, we could not find a fitting location. Time was ticking, no place was open on the night we had secured the program participants, but time was getting short. To keep things on schedule, we ended up sending out a save-the-date postcard without a location identified. People seemed to enjoy calling the organization, feeling they had found an error, pointing out how we forgot to include the location. Interestingly, not one person who gleefully called about the perceived misprint actually attended the dinner. While they did not join us, at least we know that we got noticed.

Someone has suggested, *Organize or Agonize*. Either organize a timeline to keep yourself and others on schedule or agonize the last few weeks and days leading up to the event.

Overall, anywhere from two years to 6 months out, you need to get the critical components in place. Namely, you need the program participants, the venue, and the meal. Additionally, promotional material can be prepared, but you will still need to sit on it until you are closer to the event.

This is the order that I would recommend:

2 years to 6 months

- ☐ Set your goals
- ☐ Pick a date
- ☐ Choose your venue
- ☐ Develop a theme
- ☐ Secure a speaker, musical act, or entertainment
- ☐ Plan your menu
- ☐ Produce promotional material
- ☐ Design table centerpieces and decorations
- ☐ Order, if necessary, any rental equipment (such as flatware or tablecloths)

4 months

- ☐ If not already in place, begin monthly meetings

3 months

- ☐ Mail out Save-the-Date card

10 weeks

- ☐ Begin to secure table hosts and hostesses, individuals and couples responsible for filling tables

8 weeks

- ☐ Invitations
- ☐ E-mail tables hosts and hostesses, sending digital copy of invitation

6 weeks

- ☐ E-mail/text entire mailing list with option to RSVP

5 weeks

- ☐ Distribute press releases and public service announcements

4 weeks

- ☐ Send out an organizational newsletter highlighting the dinner and reminding people on mailing list to RSVP soon
- ☐ Make contact with table hosts, offering ongoing encouragement and instructions
- ☐ Plan minute by minute details for the program
- ☐ Accumulate items necessary for the night of the dinner
  - o Organization Displays
  - o Banners
  - o Centerpieces
  - o Room Decorations
  - o Table Numbers
  - o Nametags
  - o Large envelopes to hold pledge material
  - o SASE for gifts and pledges
  - o Pledge cards
  - o Pens
- ☐ Design and print programs or any other literature for the evening
- ☐ Meet, skype, or phone all program participants including committee, venue, caterer, speaker, and entertainers
- ☐ Distribute posters, promotional material, and bulletin inserts to area organizations, businesses, and churches

2 weeks

- ☐ Mail programs and organizational literature to program participants
- ☐ Send final E-mail appeal to table hosts and prospect list

1 week

- ☐ Collect names of guests from table hosts and hostesses
- ☐ Arrange seating and print nametags
- ☐ Contact caterer and venue with final count

- 1 week

□ Thank donors, volunteers, and guests well, giving report of the results

10 FINAL THOUGHTS

Now that you have the momentum, keep it going, especially while the ideas are still fresh. Also, getting your printing designed early on will make life easier for your designers who never enjoy hearing the phrase, *I need it yesterday.*

When it comes to save-the-date postcards and invitations, many of the same rules apply as weddings. What is different from weddings, however, which changes the timetable for mailing deadlines, is that most people will not treat the evening as an "A" list event on their calendar. Someone may plan a whole vacation around their niece getting married, but people will attend a fund-raising dinner <u>if</u> they have no other plans and <u>if</u> they cannot come up with a better excuse why they cannot. You want practice due diligence, removing perceptions of disorganization and any excuses for not attending that can be blamed on you. Many people, however, will not decide to attend until literally the last week. Others will RSVP positively almost immediately, only to very casually back out at a very late date.

Overall, while wedding planners may recommend six to eight

months out for the save-the-date postcards, fund-raising dinners are probably more effective around 90 days before the event.

Included on your postcard, in order of priority and prominence, should be:

- The date and time of the event
- The planned speaker, musical group, or entertainment
- Organizational/contact information
- The location
- Opportunity to reserve a whole table or to become a table host or hostess

Of course, this is your first chance to begin to build the theme through both images and color, and you should give the designer a clear idea of what you envision. If local designers are not available, the internet has opened up the door for anyone to shop globally and for good design work to be very affordable.

Assuming you have a mailing list of at least a couple thousand names and addresses, your best value is getting the postcards printed online with a national company. The local printers who do not have the advantage of volume and *gang runs* cannot even compete in price. If you monitor a website during the year or pay attention to their email advertising, they often offer deep discounts on certain items at random times or, at the very minimum, free shipping. Most will let you purchase and pay during the sale, even if it is months before you need them or even send in the artwork.

Depending upon who is doing your mailing services, be careful about not getting the backside coated where the addresses are printed. Most companies do not have the equipment to inkjet or print addresses directly on cards with a glossy coating. If self-adhesive labels are needed because of the coating, needless material and labor costs are created. The clear coating on the front steps up the quality, but a matte finish on the back will make them easier to handle, stack, bundle, and address.

Assuming you are mailing not for profit and with a USPS permit, the mailing indicia can be printed directly on the card at either the main printing or when the addresses are inkjetted. My personal preference and the combination that has gotten the best response is inkjetting the names in a cursive, hand-writing like type and applying not-for-profit precanceled stamps. This, however, is only available to those who have a not-for-profit mailing permit with the post office or who work with a mailing company that has one.

Bottom line, try to make the save-the-date cards look as personal as possible.

The invitation, however, should be designed to be mailed out in an envelope and follow the same procedure of using precanceled stamps and cursive type on the envelope.

In addition to the information on the save-the-date postcard, the invitation design should include:

- ☐ Map to the venue
- ☐ RSVP date with clear instructions and multiple ways to respond
- ☐ Biography of speaker or program participants

Even if you are still a year out, go ahead and get the design work completed. Printing can wait for now. Not wanting to handle or store the material, plan the actual printing so that it can be shipped directly to the mailing services company to arrive about the time they are ready to prepare it for the post office.

During this time, do not forget to use the digital copies of the design work to include with emails, online invitations, or on your organization's website page. You also want to print extra save-the-date cards and/or invitations to distribute widely to volunteers or people interested in the organization.

As a side note, depending upon the criteria used for your mailing list, you may discover gaps in who receives the mailings. Devise a good plan to close those gaps. Organizational mailing lists, to stay current, are often drawn from recent donors. If the criteria for your invitation mailing list, for instance, includes "individuals who have given over $50 in the past three years," you may find that some people that love your organization are unintentionally overlooked and not included. For example, many volunteers who sacrifice much time and regularly share in some form of in-kind giving would not make your mailing list criteria cut.

On the other hand, do not forget that the purpose of the night is to raise funds. This is the only wat to ensure that those dedicated volunteers still have a place to serve and that services can still be provided. Knowing who to exclude from the invitation list may be as important as knowing who to include. Everyone who has given a donation and everyone who has volunteered some time are not always the best prospects for the guests of a successful dinner.

The goal is to produce the most quality promotional material possible to get the word to the most qualified invitees.

Conclusion

Each time we finish a dinner and drive away with a van full of left over promotional material, a few rental items to return, and an envelope full of pledges and donations, the exhaustion is only eclipsed by the mixed feelings of intense gratitude and fear that we could never top this event again.

Like a wedding ceremony, however, that may take months and months to plan and is over so quickly, it is really only the beginning. New relationships are formed at the dinner and many of the guests will become lifelong donors, volunteers, or otherwise partners in the cause.

Fundraising dinners and events work. There may be times where you wonder if they are worth the effort, but be certain that not doing them always brings the same results, or lack of results. Few activities have more of a win-win outcome where the organization is genuinely helped and donors have a sincerely good time.

THE FUNDRAISING DINNER

ABOUT THE AUTHOR

Phil Wood organized and filed for his first 501(c)3 as a young man in his mid-twenties. Since then, he has continually served as a Trustee, Board Member, Employee, or Volunteer at churches, not-for-profit organizations and agencies. Fund raising, by default and as a necessity, has remained a primary focus.

53410948R00029

Made in the USA
Lexington, KY
03 July 2016